THE BRAIN DIET

An Essential Guide to Amazing Foods and Supplements That Fight Neurological Disorders

BY

Nicholas J. Bennett

Copyright

Dedication

This book is dedicated to people out there with neurological issues and to you, you will be found and so your loved ones.

Table of Contents

INTRODUCTION

We might believe that we have a few infections or infirmities that are brought about by maturing. Age-related infections can be forestalled on the off chance that we deal with our eating regimen by eating supplement thick food varieties and being dynamic. We want to plant food varieties for our physical and mental prosperity. Many individuals don't comprehend the benefit of consuming vegetables and foods grown from the ground they ought to be remembered for our day-to-day diet. Cancer prevention agents, for example, polyphenols, phytochemicals, and phytonutrients found in foods grown from the ground are advantageous to our wellbeing by advancing the ORAC esteem.

The Oxygen Revolutionary Absorbance Limit or ORAC esteem is a rating framework created by the Public Establishment on Maturing and the Public Foundations of Wellbeing to quantify the cell reinforcement limit of different food varieties. Food varieties with high ORAC values mean high cancer prevention agent limits and food varieties are successful at killing free revolutionaries that cause oxidative pressure that is destructive to our bodies. The cancer prevention agent upsides of the food varieties recorded are communicated in ORAC (Oxygen Revolutionary Absorbance Limit) units.

You can look for food varieties sequentially to find their ORAC values, or on the other hand, if you need to go directly to the best cell reinforcement and are hostile to maturing "superfoods. Similarly as competitors take enhancements to work on their actual execution, certain individuals expect to hone their knowledge with purported "cerebrum enhancers." obviously, no pill can cause you a virtuoso except if you too would one day, so is a mind enhancer? It can mean a few things. It can mean spices or supplements that further develop reliability, sharpness, centre, fixation, memory and even state of mind. Frequently, individuals will see that they are more engaged and alert, they are more propelled, and they process data quicker. Cerebrum supporters might seem to animate mental movement, however, they are not energizers in the severe sense like things like caffeine, ephedrine or amphetamines. More often than nobody knows how they work.

WHAT ARE ORAC UNITS?

The ORAC (Oxygen Revolutionary Absorbance Limit) unit, ORAC esteem or "ORAC score" is a technique for estimating the cell reinforcement limit of different food varieties and enhancements. Estimation in vivo (significance inside the human body) is beyond the realm of possibilities. Consequently, the specific connection between the ORAC worth of a food/supplement and the subsequent thought medical advantages has not been demonstrated. Notwithstanding, numerous researchers hypothesize that food varieties high on the ORAC scale might be more compelling at killing free revolutionaries. Albeit the free extreme hypothesis of maturing is problematic, this might slow oxidative cycles and free extreme harm that can add to progress in years related cerebrum degeneration and sickness.

PART 1-THE STOMACH CEREBRUM SENTIMENT

Is it true or not that you know all about the stomach cerebrum pivot? On the off chance that you've at any point felt 'butterflies' at seeing a friend or family member or lost your craving when you've been worried, you may know that your psyche and stomach are associated. Be that as it may, the stomach cerebrum pivot is a genuine peculiarity, and this consistent two-way correspondence, when noticeably off, can set off stomach and other wellbeing-related issues.

Overall, the stomach cerebrum pivot is a correspondence framework between the mind and the trillions of microscopic organisms, parasites and infections living inside your digestion tracts. Different investigations have demonstrated the way that the organization of stomach microorganisms can significantly affect psychological well-being and the working of the sensory system. A sound eating regimen assumes a critical part in forming this microbiome by advancing the development of valuable microscopic organisms and halting the collection of destructive ones. Nourishment can likewise impact correspondence along the stomach cerebrum pivot, further influencing the connections between the gastrointestinal parcel and the sensory system.

The stomach microbiome is a significant piece of this stomach cerebrum association. It grows at the same time as the focal sensory system and has a strong impact on numerous different mental cycles. During dysbiosis, the stomach cerebrum pivot pathways are dysregulated, which can make the actual obstruction between the focal sensory system and the cardiovascular framework more permeable. At the point when this blood-cerebrum obstruction is spilling, it might prompt aggravation of the mind matter. Stomach-related neuroinflammation has been connected to the improvement of sicknesses like different sclerosis, stroke, Alzheimer's infection and Parkinson's illness.

THE VAGUS NERVE

The human stomach contains almost 500 million neurons, which are associated with the cerebrum through nerves. The vagus nerve is one of the greatest nerves associating your gastrointestinal parcel to your sensory system and assumes numerous significant parts in your body. It ranging affects aggravation and the microbiota organization in the stomach, yet many variables can influence how well it capabilities. Mental pressure, for instance, significantly affects the vagus nerve and is associated with the advancement of gastrointestinal problems like bad temper entrails condition and provocative inside infection.

SYNAPSES

Your stomach and your cerebrum additionally convey through synthetic substances called synapses. Synapses combined by the cerebrum are associated with controlling feelings and the 'instinctive reaction. Studies have shown that these mixtures may likewise assume a significant part of the stomach. Synapses of norepinephrine, epinephrine, dopamine, and serotonin can direct and control the bloodstream, yet additionally, influence solid discharges, supplement assimilation, gastrointestinal insusceptible framework, and the microbiome. Numerous synapses answerable for keeping up with our psychological well-being, are delivered either by the stomach cells or by the stomach microorganisms.

SYNTHETIC SUBSTANCES DELIVERED BY STOMACH MICROORGANISMS

Stomach microorganisms make up various synthetic substances that influence how our cerebrum's capability. Bacterial maturation of dietary fibre is the fundamental wellspring of short-chain unsaturated fats (SCFA, for example, butyrate, propionate and acetic acid derivation. These mixtures have been displayed to forestall stomach-related issues and decrease the gamble of creating corpulence and type 2 diabetes. Short-chain unsaturated fats can relocate across the blood-cerebrum obstruction and subsequently affect mind construction and capability. Unfortunate stomach well-being might add to the beginning and movement of discouragement, nervousness, schizophrenia, chemical imbalance range problems, headache, and epilepsy.

There is a critical connection between the stomach cerebrum pivot and that we are so defenceless to stretch as well. Persistent pressure can set off episodes of discouragement and nervousness. It's been hypothesized that individuals who have great stomach well-being might be stronger to tension than the people who battle with it. Different examinations have additionally shown how early-life changes to the stomach microbiota via anti-microbial openness, absence of breastfeeding, birth by C-segment, disease, stress openness, and other ecological impacts can bring about long-haul modifications of stress-related physiology and conduct.

THE STOMACH AS THE SUBSEQUENT CEREBRUM

Our stomach microbiota assumes a fundamental part in our physical and mental wellbeing using its brain organization: the intestinal sensory system (ENS), a mind-boggling arrangement of around 100 million nerves tracked down in the covering of the stomach. The ENS is some of the time called the "second cerebrum," and it emerges from similar tissues as our focal sensory system (CNS) during the fetal turn of events. In this manner, it has numerous underlying and synthetic equals to the cerebrum. Our ENS doesn't wax philosophical or settle on leader choices like the dark sparkling hill in our skulls. However, in a supernaturally coordinated orchestra of chemicals, synapses, and electrical driving forces through a pathway of nerves, both "cerebrums" convey this way and that. These pathways incorporate and include endocrine, insusceptible, and brain connections.

Considering how intently the stomach and cerebrum communicate, it has become certain that close to home and psychosocial variables can set off side effects in the stomach. This is particularly evident in situations when the stomach is misbehaving and there's no conspicuous actual reason. Utilitarian gastrointestinal issues (FGIDs) are a gathering of more than 20 persistent and difficult-to-treat ailments of the gastrointestinal parcel that comprise an enormous extent of the introducing issues seen in clinical gastroenterology. While FGIDs were once remembered to have side effects be part of the way "in one's mind," a more exact conceptualization of these challenges places that psychosocial factors impact the genuine physiology of the stomach, as well as the regulation of. At the end of the day, mental variables can influence actual elements, similar to the development and constrictions of the GI parcel, causing, aggravation, torment, and other entrails side effects.

Considering this new getting it, it very well may be difficult to recuperate FGIDs disregarding the effect of pressure and feeling. Studies have shown that patients who attempted mentally based approaches had more noteworthy improvement in their side effects contrasted and patients who got traditional clinical treatment. The other way around, unfortunate stomach well-being has been embroiled in neurological and neuropsychiatric problems. Aggravations in stomach wellbeing have been connected to different sclerosis, mentally unbalanced range problems, and Parkinson's sickness. This is possibly connected with supportive provocative states inspired by a stomach dysbiosis-microbial lopsidedness on or inside the body. Extra associations between age-related stomach changes and Alzheimer's infection have additionally been made. Our cerebrum's well-being, which will be talked about in more profundity, is reliant upon numerous way of life decisions that intervene stomach wellbeing; including most outstanding eating routine (i.e., a decrease of an overabundance of sugar and refined starches) and pre-and probiotic consumption.

We are presently confronted with the chance of both counteraction and treatment of neurological/neuropsychiatric challenges using appropriate stomach wellbeing. On the other side, stress decreases and other mental medicines can help forestall and treat gastrointestinal problems. This revelation might prompt diminished horribleness, debilitation, and persistent reliance on medical services assets. The most engaging part of the stomach cerebrum association is the comprehension that a significant number of our day-to-day way of life decisions assume a part in intervening in our general wellbeing. This entire body's way to deal with medical services and well-being keeps on showing its worth in our life span, prosperity, and personal satisfaction: both physical and psychological well-being remain closely connected.

PART 2 – DEPRESSION; PROBIOTICS AND OMEGA-3

Omega-3 unsaturated fats are extraordinarily significant for their many capabilities inside the body. It's been read up completely for its consequences for heart wellbeing and aggravation — and, surprisingly, psychological well-being.

So what do we be aware of?

For more than 10 years, specialists have been concentrating on the impacts omega-3 might have on depression, as well as other mental and conduct conditions. Albeit the exploration is genuinely later and all the more should be finished before definite ends can be made, it's been promising. Most examinations are showing that omega-3s might be useful in treating a few types of discouragement.

There are three fundamental sorts of omega-3s in the eating routine, and two are found in fish oil: DHA (docosahexaenoic corrosive) and EPA (eicosapentaenoic corrosive). You can get fish oil by remembering fish for your eating regimen or through an enhancement. Counting fish oil and omega-3s as a component of a sound eating routine has been displayed to improve or, at times, forestall a few medical issues, including coronary illness, rheumatoid joint inflammation, and elevated cholesterol. Different circumstances are being investigated and appear as though they may likewise be assisted with omega-3 and fish oil. These incorporate ADHD as well as certain types of malignant growth. It's great to take note that fish oil and cod liver oil isn't the same thing. Fish oil doesn't contain different nutrients like D and A.

Your cerebrum needs the sort of unsaturated fats that are in omega-3s for appropriate working. It's accepted by a few that individuals who experience depression might not have sufficient EPA and DHA. This is the reason that specialists are utilizing as they concentrate on the potential advantages of utilizing omega-3 and fish oil to treat discouragement. In general, the examination done so far appears to be positive for the utilization of fish oil and omega-3s in the treatment and the executives of discouragement. Be that as it may, most investigations recognize the requirement for bigger examinations and proceeded with research regarding the matter.

Omega-3 unsaturated fats are found fundamentally in fish oil and certain marine green growth. Since discouragement shows up more uncommon in countries where individuals eat a lot of fish, researchers have explored whether fish oils might forestall or potentially treat wretchedness and another state of mind problems. Two omega-3 unsaturated fats — eicosapentaenoic corrosive (EPA) and docosahexaenoic corrosive (DHA) — are remembered to have the most potential to help individuals with state of mind problems.

HOW SHOULD OMEGA-3S FURTHER DEVELOP DEPRESSION?

Various instruments of activity have been proposed. For instance, omega-3s can undoubtedly go through the synapse layer and collaborate with the state of mind-related particles inside the cerebrum. They additionally have mitigating activities that might assist with alleviating depression.

Omega-3s have been concentrated on in different state of mind problems, like post-pregnancy anxiety, for certain promising outcomes. In bipolar confusion (hyper depression), the omega-3s might be best for the depressed stage as opposed to the hyper period of the sickness. The omega-3s have additionally been proposed to mitigate or forestall other mental circumstances including schizophrenia, marginal behavioural conditions, over-the-top enthusiastic problem, and a lack of ability to concentrate consistently jumble. Be that as it may, there is as yet insufficient proof to suggest the omega-3s in these circumstances.

WHAT DOSE OF OMEGA-3S IS ADVANTAGEOUS?

Doses for depression range from under 1 g/day to 10 g/day, however, most investigations use dosages somewhere in the range of 1 and 2 g/day. In my training, I prescribe 1 to 2 g/day of an EPA+DHA blend, with somewhere around 60% EPA, for significant depression. I'm more mindful in patients with bipolar depression because the omega-3s might welcome craziness, as can most antidepressants. In these people, I suggest utilizing omega-3 circumspectly, and ideally in blend with a solution state of mind stabilizer.

Other than fat tissue (muscle to fat ratio), the cerebrum is one of the organs that has the most fat. Not at all like a muscle to fat ratio, be that as it may, cerebrum fats don't store or deliver energy. They work for the most part to help the cerebral layers, nerve flagging, and the adjustment of quality articulation (recovery). All organelles and cells in the cerebrum rely upon polyunsaturated Omega-3 unsaturated fats. In our focal sensory system, one unsaturated fat in three is polyunsaturated. For this reason, cerebrum wellbeing relies upon us devouring food varieties wealthy in Omega-3. Since Omega-3 Fat is a fundamental piece of the focal sensory system (CNS) layer, it is indispensable to the sound capability and construction of synapses. The presence of adequate Omega-3 unsaturated fats can further develop cell layer smoothness. Having ideal smoothness is fundamental for cell correspondence.

AGGRAVATION, DEPRESSION AND OMEGA-3 UNSATURATED FAT

Depression has been believed to be brought about by a lack of monoamine neurochemicals in the body, especially serotonin and norepinephrine. Notwithstanding, developing proof backs that a types of depression might be because of predictable poor quality irritation in the body. Various examinations have connected depression with an expansion in provocative markers, explicitly cytokines. These cytokines, which incorporate growth putrefaction factor-alpha, interleukin-1 beta, and interferon, can affect the focal sensory system (CNS). A portion of the components of these cytokines incorporates diminished accessibility of synapse forerunner, changes in the digestion of synapses, and enactment of the hypothalamic-pituitary pivot - the focal pressure reaction arrangement of the body. Mental pressure can likewise hoist the levels of these cytokines. At the end of the day, these are the trouble makers remembered to be behind to depression and different infections.

Omega-3 unsaturated fats are the legends in this story. Omega-3 fats, EPA (Eicosapentaenoic corrosive) specifically, are demonstrated to have an inhibitory impact against cytokines. Moreover, it has been found that the mitigating job of Omega-3 unsaturated fat might influence cerebrum determined neurotrophic factor (BDNF), which is diminished in level in individuals with discouragement. BDNF is a neuropeptide that advances the development and endurance of synapses.

PART 3- FERMENTED FOOD; A REMEDY FOR ANXIETY

WHAT HAVE FERMENTED FOOD VARIETIES?

Fermented food varieties are food varieties that have gone through a characteristic lactofermentation process. This is when microscopic organisms devour the sugars and starch in food, transforming it into lactic corrosive. Subsequently, the food is safeguarded - and gives you a decent sound portion of probiotics. Fermented food varieties incorporate lager (not all that nutritious), yoghurt, kimchi, fermented tea, kefir, tempeh, pickles, and sauerkraut.

Fermentation is viewed as the transformation of starches to natural acids utilizing yeast and additionally microscopic organisms. During the fermentation interaction, a large number of minuscule microorganisms become implanted with the food so that when devoured, those microscopic organisms enter your stomach. While all the well-being impacts related to utilization fermentation of food varieties stay obscure, most proof recommends that customary utilization could be helpful for ideal neurophysiological working. All through the advancement of humankind, matured food varieties were devoured consistently frequently due to legitimate need. A long period prior, people didn't have the advantage of comfortable strolling through the supermarket and looking over a large number of accessible things; they ate anything that they might find, chase, or accumulate. Generally speaking, this implied eating food varieties that had matured like spoiled natural products.

Maybe a significant issue with westernized consuming fewer calories is that most food is completely cleaned and disinfected to the point that all (possibly important) microorganisms from fermentation are destroyed. This implies that except if you are eating matured food varieties consistently, your stomach well-being might be less than ideal. The new examination additionally recommends that your psychological well-being might be more unfortunate also, with one review taking note that expanded fermented food utilization could diminish social nervousness.

FERMENTED FOOD VARIETIES FOR A SOUND STOMACH AND GENERALLY SPEAKING WELLBEING

Regardless of whether you understand it, fermentation is an interaction that is utilized to deliver a portion of the world's number one food varieties and refreshments. What are a few fermented food varieties? Well-known matured food varieties incorporate things like wine, lager, yoghurt, particular fermented cheeses, and, surprisingly, chocolate and espresso. One of the most well-known matured food varieties universally is yoghurt, which has been devoured in specific regions of the planet for millennia, alongside firmly related kefir. Over the entire course of time, maturing food varieties provided our predecessors with the choice of dragging out the newness of grains, vegetables and milk that were accessible to them during various seasons.

It's moderately easy to make an enormous cluster of matured food varieties to have prepared to eat in your cooler — in addition, they ought to keep going seemingly forever because of the valuable microscopic organisms they contain. Eating fermented (or "refined") food varieties is the most helpful method for getting a day-to-day portion of probiotic microorganisms that help stomach well-being and that's only the tip of the iceberg.

A portion of the numerous ways these food varieties support generally speaking well-being incorporate by:

- Further developing assimilation and mental capability
- Supporting insusceptibility
- Helping treat bad temper entailed infection
- Giving minerals that form bone thickness
- Helping battle sensitivities
- Killing destructive yeast and microorganisms

RUNDOWN OF PROBABLY THE BEST-MATURED FOOD VARIETIES TO REMEMBER FOR YOUR EATING REGIMEN:

Kefir

Kefir is a matured milk item (produced using cow, goat or sheep's milk) that is preferences like a drinkable yoghurt. Kefir benefits incorporate giving elevated degrees of vitamin B12, calcium, magnesium, nutrient K2, biotin, folate, compounds and probiotics. Kefir has been consumed for above and beyond 3,000 years. The term kefir was begun in Russia and Turkey and signifies "feeling significantly better."

Fermented tea

Fermented tea is a matured beverage made of dark tea and sugar (from different sources like natural sweeteners, natural products or honey). It contains a settlement of microscopic organisms and yeast that is liable for starting the maturation interaction once joined with sugar. Do matured food varieties like fermented tea contain liquor? Fermented tea has followed measures of liquor however excessively little to make inebriation or even be recognizable. Other matured food varieties, like yoghurt or aged veggies, regularly have no liquor by any stretch of the imagination.

Sauerkraut

Sauerkraut is quite possibly of the most established conventional food, with extremely lengthy roots in German, Russian and Chinese cooking, going back 2,000 years or more. Sauerkraut signifies "acrid cabbage" in German, albeit the Germans weren't quick to make sauerkraut from fermented green or red cabbage. Sauerkraut is high in fiber, vitamin A, L-ascorbic acid, vitamin K, and B nutrients. It's likewise an extraordinary wellspring of iron, copper, calcium, sodium, manganese and magnesium. Genuine, conventional, matured sauerkraut should be refrigerated, is generally put away in glass containers and says that it is aged on the bundle/name.

Pickles

Didn't imagine that pickles had probiotics? Matured pickles contain ton nutrients and minerals, in addition to cell reinforcements and stomach fermented well-disposed probiotic microscopic organisms. Most locally acquired pickles are made with vinegar and cucumbers, and albeit this makes the pickles taste harsh, this doesn't prompt regular maturation. Fermented pickles ought to be made with cucumbers and saline solution. What is the best-fermented brand of pickles on the off chance that you need probiotics? While picking a container of pickles, search for "lactic corrosive matured pickles" made by a producer that utilizes natural items and saline solution, refrigerates the pickles, and expresses that the pickles have matured. On the off chance that you can track down a neighbourhood producer, for example, at a rancher's market, you'll get probably the best probiotics for your wellbeing.

Miso

Miso is made by maturing soybeans, grain or earthy colored rice with koji, a sort of parasite. It's a conventional Japanese fixing in recipes including miso soup. It's been a staple in Chinese and Japanese weight control plans for roughly 2,500 years.

Tempeh

One more valuable fermented food made with soybeans is tempeh, an item that is made by consolidating soybeans with a tempeh starter (which is a blend of live shape). At the point when it sits for a little while, this results in it turns into a thick, cake-like item that contains the two probiotics and a powerful portion of protein as well. Tempeh is like tofu however not as elastic and that's only the tip of the iceberg "grainy."

Natto

Natto is a well-known food in Japan comprising of matured soybeans. It is some of the time even had for breakfast in Japan and ordinarily joined with soy sauce, karashi mustard and Japanese clustering onion. After fermentation, it fosters serious areas of strength for a profound flavour and tacky, disgusting surface that not every person who is new to natto appreciates.

Kimchi

Kimchi is a conventional matured Korean dish that is produced using vegetables, including cabbage, in addition to flavors like ginger, garlic, pepper and other flavoring. It's frequently added to Korean recipes like rice bowls, ramen or bibimbap.

Crude Cheddar

Crude milk cheeses are made with milk that hasn't been sanitized. Goat milk, sheep milk and A2 cow's delicate cheeses are especially high in probiotics, including *thermophillus, Bifidus, bulgaricus and acidophilus*. To view them as genuinely matured/matured cheeses, read the fixing name and search for cheddar that has not been sanitized. The name ought to demonstrate that the cheddar is crude and has been matured for a considerable length of time or more.

Yogurt

Yoghurt and kefir are one-of-a-kind dairy items since they are exceptionally accessible and a portion of the top probiotic food varieties that many individuals eat consistently. Probiotic yoghurt is presently the most consumed matured dairy item in the US and numerous other industrialized countries as well. It's prescribed while purchasing yoghurt to search for three things:

It comes from goat or sheep milk on the off chance that you experience difficulty processing cow's milk.

It's produced using the milk of creatures that have been grass-taken care of.

It's natural.

Apple Juice Vinegar

Apple juice vinegar contains a few probiotics. It additionally contains particular kinds of acids like acidic corrosive, which upholds the capability of probiotics and prebiotics in your stomach. Be that as it may, most vinegar accessible in the general store doesn't contain probiotics. You can add one tablespoon of apple juice vinegar to a beverage two times every day. Before breakfast and lunch or breakfast and supper, add one tablespoon of apple juice vinegar to your dinner, and afterwards, begin polishing off additional matured vegetables like sauerkraut and kimchi or drinking kvass to truly support probiotic levels.

Kvass

Kvass is a conventional matured refreshment that has a comparative taste to lager. Similar to fermented tea, it goes through a fermentation interaction and contains probiotics. It's produced using lifeless, sourdough rye bread and is viewed as a non-cocktail since it contains just around 0.5 per cent to 1 per cent liquor. The more it matures, the more defenseless it is to turn out to be a heavier drinker. On the off chance that you've never tasted kvass, it has a tart, natural, pungent flavor and can be a mixed bag. Some of the time it is fermented with flavors from organic products and spices to make it seriously engaging.

Sourdough Bread

Certain customarily made bread, for example, genuine sourdough bread, are matured, however, they don't contain probiotics. Maturation helps make supplements found in the grains more accessible for assimilation and diminishes antinutrient content that might make processing troublesome.

Curds

Since more exploration is affirming that probiotics are exceptionally advantageous, food producers are starting to make probiotic dairy items, for example, curds all the more promptly accessible. Like yoghurt, curds can be matured when microscopic organisms assist with separating the lactose (a kind of sugar) in the dairy. While buying curds, search for brands that are low in sugar and that contain dynamic societies. A few kinds are likewise called dry curd curds or rancher's cheddar.

Coconut Kefir

For individuals who can't endure dairy, coconut kefir is an extraordinary other option. This probiotic-rich beverage is made with velvety coconut milk and kefir grains, however, not at all like customary kefir or yoghurt it's sans dairy and veggie lovers well dispose of. Attempt it

PART 4 - BERRIES FOR PTSD

Post-Traumatic Stress Disorder (PTSD)

PTSD is a psychological well-being condition that can be brought about by a terrifying or hazardous occasion. Initially a term used to portray the damaged condition of some returning conflict veterans, it is currently perceived that different horrendous circumstances can cause PTSD, for example, mishaps, wrongdoing, catastrophes, labor or family or accomplice misuse. In the wake of encountering what is happening individuals can have unmistakable inclinations of frenzy, outrage or recollect distinctive pictures, but most frequently these sensations blur following a couple of months. Anyway it is assessed that 20% of individuals who experience an injury can go onto foster PTSD, where these side effects persevere.

SIDE EFFECTS OF PTSD

Frequently individuals experience the ill effects of flashbacks, distinctive bad dreams or undesirable recollections. They might feel hypervigilant in their regular day to day existences, specific assuming there are sounds, sights or scents that help them to remember the occurrence. This can likewise prompt avoidant conduct, not going to specific places or staying away from circumstances. Whenever set off by something in their current circumstance that associates them to the horrendous memory, they can either feel suffused with alarm, dread, disgrace or outrage, or similarly feel cut off from feelings and experience deadness and disassociation.

WHAT CAUSES PTSD?

Why an individual creates PTSD isn't completely perceived. It can for instance connect with the time allotment the injury persevered, or the seriousness of the experience. There is a proof to recommend hereditary defenselessness assumes a part, yet similarly how much help an individual gets from their loved ones has been displayed to enhance its turn of events. The rehashed 'hyperarousal' that the singular encounters after the occasion recommends that it very well might be the bodies over cautious approach to reminding them to remain safe. Anyway this suffusion of the pressure chemicals cortisol and adrenaline, are troubling for the person as well as the persevering arrival of stress chemicals have potentially negative side-effects to their wellbeing.

Berries, for example, blueberries, raspberries, raspberries and strawberries have so many medical advantages, including however not restricted to working on mental capability, offering benefits for PTSD, diminishing aggravation and, surprisingly, expanding great microscopic organisms in our stomach. There are even beginning promising consequences of a compound in blackberries having anti-infection like properties against drug-safe microscopic organisms MRSA (*methicillin safe staphylococcus aureus*).

BLUEBERRIES SUPPORT SEROTONIN AND STRAIGHTFORWARDNESS PTSD

Blueberries support serotonin and may assist with PTSD and nervousness. This could help on the off chance that you have nervousness and discouragement as well, since low serotonin is much of the time one of the fundamental variables. We realize that irritation assumes a part in state of mind issues so this is one more component for supporting your body healthfully.

Wild blueberries are a rich wellspring of polyphenols, fiber and different mixtures that are processed by the gastrointestinal microbiota.

Various investigations are showing the advantages of Bifidobacterium probiotics on state of mind and nervousness. The following are a couple of them:

- Diminished burdensome side effects in IBS patients
- Diminished nervousness (creature study)
- Diminished irritation, adjusted synapses and a positive effect on the HPA pivot (creature study)
- Blackberry compound as an anti-infection against MRSA?

This segment doesn't include eating blackberries however I'm including it since I simply love this story, it's motivating and it has not gotten any inclusion in the established press. An article in a neighborhood distribution reports that Irish high schooler wins top science prize for blackberry anti-microbial that battles safe microscopic organisms

PART 5 - ATTENTION DEFICIT DISORDER AND LACTOSE INTOLERANCE

A lack of ability to concentrate consistently (ADD) is portrayed by distractibility and challenges overseeing time, coordinating and thinking. At the point when an individual is likewise exceptionally dynamic, the condition is called attention deficiency hyperactivity disorder (ADHD). People with ADD are known to be defenseless against food sensitivities and dairy items top the rundown of known allergens that might cause these side effects.

THE ISSUE WITH MILK

Milk is comprised of numerous proteins however the two significant suspects that cause sensitivities are whey and casein. Whey is the watery substance that is isolated out while making cheddar and casein is transformed into "curds" during this interaction. Certain individuals are "lactose narrow minded," and that implies that they experience issues processing milk items. This is not quite the same as a sensitivity, which can be hazardous 2. Side effects of milk sensitivities incorporate stomach torment, wheezing, skin issues and queasiness. Studies have additionally shown that the evacuation of milk, explicitly casein from the eating routine has diminished hyperactivity and impulsivity in youngsters with ADHD.

LACTOSE NARROW MINDEDNESS

Lactose is a catalyst used to process the sugar lactose. Individuals with lactose narrow mindedness have a lack in this compound. Side effects of lactose narrow mindedness incorporate irritated stomach, gas, swelling and looseness of the bowels. Lactose narrow mindedness is not a resistant reaction that outcomes in aggravation, setting off the development of antibodies. Be that as it may, milk sensitivities might harm the stomach related framework, causing a lack in lactose, in this manner causing lactose narrow mindedness.

DISTINGUISHING MILK SENSITIVITIES

Milk sensitivities might be suspect in light of side effects that eruption during utilization. Be that as it may, responsive qualities or sensitivities cannot entirely set in stone by utilizing a disposal diet where milk is dispensed with for five to seven days. Then, at that point, it is once again introduced watching to check whether side effects show up. A doctor can play out a blood test which is more secure than the disposal diet on the off chance that there is a gamble of serious response upon milk renewed introduction. A skin test can likewise aid determination. This includes setting the food allergen under the skin and noticing the response. A few people respond to an allergen promptly empowering a determination in light of a blood or skin test. Be that as it may, the greater part the small kids with milk sensitivities have a postponed response wherein case, the disposal test would be a more precise demonstrative instrument.

MAKING A WITHOUT DAIRY DIET

Casein is tracked down in the entirety of warm blooded creature's milk so goats, sheep's and, surprisingly, human bosom milk can set off unfavorably susceptible responses. Casein is likewise utilized in numerous food varieties as a limiting specialist, so one requirements to painstakingly peruse the marks or shop at a wellbeing food store that sells food items explicitly for clients with dietary limitations. There are various without casein cook books available and in any event, cooking classes. People who don't eat dairy items ought to ensure that they get satisfactory protein and calcium through different sources, for example,

- Tofu
- Eggs
- Mixed greens
- Vegetables
- Entire grains
- Strengthened cereals

YOUNGSTERS AND FOOD SENSITIVITIES

Youngsters on the chemical imbalance range frequently have a double determination of ADD. Food sensitivities in this populace are exceptionally normal and there have been reports of promising outcomes when both dairy and wheat items are eliminated from the eating regimen. This diet is classified "without glutin sans casein" (GFCF). People with ADD alone or a double determination of ADD and chemical imbalance might profit from this eating routine. It is suggested that a doctor affirm any food sensitivity and a nutritionist help with planning a suitable eating routine.

Diets to stay away from include:

- Wheat
- Rye
- Grain
- Oats. Although oats without help from anyone else don't contain gluten, they are frequently handled alongside gluten-containing grains and might be polluted. Since it is challenging to say without a doubt, it's ideal to completely keep away from oats.
- Pasta
- Bread
- Flapjacks
- Saltines
- Every single prepared great
- Granola bars
- Cocoa
- Soy sauce
- Lunch get-together meats
- Grain malt
- Baking powder
- Bouillon solid shapes
- Fasteners
- Fillers

- Extenders
- HPP (hydrolyzed plant protein)
- HVP (hydrolyzed vegetable protein)
- TVP (texturized vegetable protein)
- Malto-dextrose or malt
- MSG (monosodium glutamate)
- Adjusted food starch
- Flavors
- Pastry specialist's yeast
- Vegetable gum
- Some food starches
- Casein
- All dairy items contain casein
- All types of creature milk, be they skim, low-fat, dissipated, or consolidated
- Yogurt
- All cheeses
- Margarine
- Frozen yogurt
- Milk chocolate
- Dairy items are the clearest wellsprings of casein, however milk is a fixing in numerous non-dairy arrangements.

The accompanying food things are referred to contain casein along with gluten:

- Canned soup
- Bread morsels
- Packaged salad dressings
- Soy cheddar
- Biting gum
- Breath mints
- Protein shakes
- Handled meats and frankfurters
- Wine
- Milk solids
- Whey
- Caseinate
- Sodium caseinate
- Caseinogen
- Lactose
- Hydrolyzed vegetable protein

- Non-food things
- Beauty care products, a few prescriptions, and numerous other non-food things might contain unappetizing gluten. A significant number of these things are utilized around the house consistently! They include:
- Stamps and envelopes (the tacky part)
- Multivitamins
- Numerous solution and non-prescription drugs
- A few homegrown supplements
- Lip items like lip emollient, Chap Stick, lip sparkle, or lipstick
- Cross-defilement

Keep an eye out for cross-defilement, or circumstances where food varieties with casein or gluten may unintentionally come into contact with without gluten or casein food varieties, or with the utensils your youngster utilizes. For example, you utilize a blade to margarine your toast, then, at that point, give it to your kid to use without washing it. The most effective way to stay away from cross-defilement is to have the entire family go on the GFCF diet. This will hold your youngster back from being estranged from the remainder of the family and the food varieties the person in question appreciates, and it might wind up treating obscure food prejudices in other relatives.

PART 6 - ORTHOREXIA NERVOSA; SUPPLEMENTAL REMEDIES

Orthorexia is a genuinely ongoing term that is utilized to portray a disarranged eating design characterized by the limitation of any food varieties that are emotionally considered "unfortunate." One's meaning of quality food varieties can fluctuate, but this problem ordinarily includes exclusively devouring food varieties that are natural, spotless and pure. This would incorporate crude, entire and restricted - fixing food varieties. While people ought to invest SOME energy contemplating settling on quality food decisions, permitting oneself to just devour food varieties that fulfill ideal guidelines - which is an example characteristic of somebody with orthorexia - feels denying and out of reach, which can eventually bring about sensations of responsibility or potentially disgrace.

Frequently, we see orthorexia happening co-dismally with over the top enthusiastic problem (OCD). Similarly as people with OCD set principles for how they should perform ceremonies or impulses, we are seeing people with orthorexia setting exceptionally exclusive expectations concerning diet and food utilization. On the off chance that food varieties considered "unfortunate" are devoured, considerations can frequently turn out to be upsetting to such an extent that people want to play out an impulse (which can frequently incorporate over-practicing or potentially fasting to ease nervousness). Similarly as those with OCD experience debilitation to psycho-social working, people with orthorexia frequently become disconnected as everyday undertakings can feel overpowering. Exploring shopping for food, feasting corridors/buffets, heading out to the shopping center or motion pictures, going out to eat or essentially getting a charge out of time at a companion's or relative's home can be stressors for those with orthorexia, thus they are frequently stayed away from.

Here are a few genuine instances of orthorexia cases. You will want to perceive how it mirrors contemplations and ways of behaving that are additionally connected with OCD.

- She wants to eat at a similar specific time consistently (not 5 minutes prior or later) or, in all likelihood calories will be consumed distinctively and in this manner add to diabetes, coronary illness and weight gain
- He should have vegetables at each eating episode as they are the "exemplification of wellbeing"
- They will just shop at Entire Food varieties or rancher's business sectors; other supermarkets are impossible
- He explicitly designs out the time he showers at night as a shower will assist with processing supper. The shower should be among supper and night nibble to help with sensations of completion/eating excessively near one another.

These are normal signs and side effects of orthorexia1 that have OCD attributes:

- Enthusiastic checking of fixing records and nourishing marks
- An expansion in worry about the wellbeing of fixings
- Removing a rising number of nutritional categories (all sugar, all starches, all dairy, all meat, every single creature item, and so forth.)
- A powerlessness to eat everything except a restricted gathering of food varieties that are considered "sound" or "unadulterated"
- Surprising interest in the soundness of what others are eating
- Going through hours out of every day contemplating what food may be served at forthcoming occasions
- Showing elevated degrees of trouble when "safe" or "solid" food varieties aren't accessible
- Over the top following of food and "solid way of life" web journals on Twitter and Instagram
- Self-perception concerns could conceivably be available

Both orthorexia and OCD are difficult circumstances that can seriously obstruct upon everyday working. An integrative specialist might suggest at least one of the accompanying ordinarily utilized supplements. Continuously converse with your doctor before taking any new enhancements.

5HTP

5-hydroxtryptophan is an antecedent of serotonin that has given help to numerous patients with OCD. The commonplace portion is 100 to 300 milligrams (mg). Now and again, portions as high as 600 mg might be required.

Vitamin B12

A lack of this serotonin-supporting B nutrient is normal in OCD. Albeit most traditional specialists consider blood levels between 200 to 1,100 picograms per milliliter (pg/mL) ordinary. On the off chance that a patient is low, he treats with week after week intramuscular B12 infusions until the blood level compasses 900 pg/mL. A few patients experience a sensational diminishing in side effects with only this treatment.

Folate

This B nutrient is significant in the assembling of serotonin, and it can support the viability of antidepressants. Be that as it may, certain individuals with OCD can't process folate as a result of a hereditary irregularity. On the off chance that you have OCD, consider having a methylenetetrahydrofolate reductase transformations (MTHFR) test to check whether you miss the mark on chemicals to deal with folate. On the off chance that the test is positive, you might have to take one to 15 grams of folate day to day.

Zinc

This mineral is a significant cofactor in the development of serotonin. A lack of zinc likewise can have various other unfortunate results for wellbeing, for example, discouragement, unfortunate digestion of fundamental unsaturated fats, lower melatonin, greater weakness to stress, and stomach related challenges. Think about a portion of 30 mg day to day.

Inositol

 In certain patients, enhancing with inositol — a nutrient like compound that influences the serotonin receptors on cells — is the main treatment required for OCD. Think about taking 5 to 10 grams (g) day to day, getting going with 1 g and expanding by 1 g week after week. Taking an excessive amount of inositol excessively fast can cause gastrointestinal inconvenience.

Omega-3 unsaturated fats

The cerebrum is 60% fat, and ideal mind capability requires sound fats, for example, the omega-3 unsaturated fats eicosapentaenoic corrosive (EPA) and docosahexaenoic corrosive (DHA) found in fish oil. Consider a day to day supplement containing 3 grams of omega-3 unsaturated fats with a marginally higher proportion of EPA to DHA.

N-acetylcysteine (NAC)

This compound is a subordinate of the amino corrosive cysteine and helps produce glutathione, a strong mitigating cell reinforcement. In a review distributed in the Diary of Clinical Psychopharmacology, 36 ladies with OCD who didn't answer serotonin-supporting prescription were partitioned into two gatherings: One gathering took NAC day to day and one gathering took a fake treatment. A sum of 53% of the NAC bunch had critical improvement in OCD side effects, contrasted and 15 percent of the fake treatment bunch. Think about taking 2 to 3 g of NAC day to day.

Glycine

This compound is a forerunner to glutamine and gamma aminobutyric corrosive (GABA), two quieting synapses that can restrain over the top reasoning. Think about taking 3 to 6 g of glycine day to day.

Vitamin D

This nutrient can bring down neuroinflammation. Your primary care physician can test you for lack of vitamin D (blood level under 30 nanograms for every milliliter [ng/ml]). On the off chance that you're insufficient, take 2,000 to 4,000 worldwide units (IU) of vitamin D day to day to carry levels to somewhere around 50 ng/ml.

Magnesium

 To cool aggravation, take 400 to 800 mg of magnesium citrate or glycinate day to day, partitioned into a few portions.

WAY OF LIFE SUPPORT

A few way of life variables can likewise influence OCD:

Unfortunate rest

Treat a sleeping disorder with further developed rest cleanliness. Head to sleep simultaneously consistently and get up simultaneously each day, giving yourself somewhere around seven hours in bed.

Stress

Stress causes aggravation as well as deteriorates the side effects of OCD. Decrease pressure by learning and rehearsing care based pressure decrease strategies.

Dispense with gluten and casein

 Individuals who are feeling the loss of the stomach related catalyst DPP-4 can't satisfactorily separate specific proteins from dairy (casein) and wheat (gluten), delivering morphine-like mixtures (casomorphin, gliadorphin) that can assume a part in OCD. Taking the DPP-4 stomach related catalyst, what separates gluten, and disposing of dairy and gluten-containing food varieties (wheat, rye, grain, and oats) some of the time fundamentally or even totally settle side effects, especially in youngsters and teenagers with OCD. The Incomparable Fields Research facility tests for casomorphin and gliadorphin in the urine

PART 7- MAGICAL DIET APPROACH TO INSOMNIA

The main source of a sleeping disorder is pressure. Stress, because of stress over your work, your funds, your connections, your youngsters, and so forth plays devastation on your adrenal organs and cerebrum. This outcomes in a powerlessness to rest around evening time, leaving you gazing at the roof or counting sheep, appealing to nod off. Fortunately, numerous regular enhancements for rest support a sleeping disorder, available without a prescription at most pharmacies, can assist with this issue without you getting up toward the beginning of the day with a hazy head.

These are a few effectively accessible regular enhancements for rest support a sleeping disorder:

Melatonin

Melatonin is a normally happening chemical inside your body delivered by the pineal organ in your cerebrum. This chemical assumes a significant part in your rest wake cycle and is generally higher during the nights and falls toward the beginning of the day. As a result of melatonin's rest controlling properties, many individuals take a chemical enhancement while encountering rest challenges. This makes it one of the go-to regular enhancements for rest support a sleeping disorder or while encountering a rest cycle interruption, for example, is the situation with individuals experiencing plane slack. It is likewise a number one of those whose work prerequisites need them to rest during the day. Albeit considered ok for use for brief periods, relatively few investigations exist about the drawn out utilization of a melatonin supplement. A melatonin supplement along with light treatment might assist those with dementia in limiting the event of fretfulness around evening time.

L-Theanine

L-theanine is an amino corrosive ordinarily tracked down in green tea. It might increment and lower your feelings of anxiety since it sets off the arrival of gamma-aminobutyric corrosive (GABA) in your cerebrum. GABA significantly affects your cerebrum's synapses and in this manner has a quieting impact. Taken as an enhancement, for example, Adrenal Stay unconscious as theanine, your body effectively retains this amino corrosive and lifts your GABA levels and regulates the other synapse levels. Theanine might bring down your circulatory strain levels, be that as it may. Thus, on the off chance that experiencing low circulatory strain, if it's not too much trouble, first converse with a medical services expert before thinking about taking this enhancement.

Glycine

Glycine is additionally one of those amino acids falling under the standard of regular enhancements for rest support a sleeping disorder. It isn't viewed as a fundamental amino corrosive because your body can make its own. It is, be that as it may, one of the structure blocks of protein. Essential glycine sources incorporate lean meat, dairy, vegetables, and fish. Other than its part in protein combination, glycine is likewise a focal sensory system inhibitory synapse. As indicated by studies, a glycine supplement might assist with working on your rest. The decision is still out on how it does this precisely, yet it might result from its part in bringing down your internal heat level around evening time, demonstrating the time has come to fall asleep. No investigations, at this point, have checked out at the proceeded, long haul utilization of glycine as an enhancement. Albeit for the most part thought a protected enhancement, certain individuals have revealed gastrointestinal incidental effects while involving glycine as an enhancement. Incidental effects incorporate gentler stools, queasiness, regurgitating, and a resentful stomach.

L-Tryptophan

L-tryptophan is a fundamental amino corrosive and assumes a part in protein combination. One concentrate on tryptophan shows that is may assist with further developing your rest quality and assist you with nodding off quicker. Found in all protein food varieties, L-tryptophan is a forerunner to both melatonin and serotonin. You ought to be cautious about immediately considering an L-tryptophan supplement because inaccurate use might make unfavorable side impacts. The incidental effects announced incorporate discombobulation, hives, queasiness, sluggishness, exhaustion, heart palpitations, loss of muscle coordination, and various others. Tryptophan may likewise slow down prescriptions. On the off chance that considering an L-tryptophan supplement, kindly first converse with your medical services professional to decide appropriateness and measurements.

5-Hydroxytryptophan (5-HTP)

5-HTP, an L-tryptophan side-effect, assists with serotonin creation. As one of the conceivable outcomes while considering regular items for rest support a sleeping disorder, individuals will generally take an enhancement like Adrenal Rest when their a sleeping disorder is connected with nervousness or discouragement. As 5-HTP converts to serotonin, it is accepted to assist with controlling state of mind and straightforwardness stress. Do observe, in any case, that taking a 5-HTP supplement along with a stimulant isn't fitting since it could cause serotonin condition. This condition has a few side effects that incorporate disarray, quakes, unpredictable heartbeat, visualizations, and hypertension. Kindly first converse with your medical services professional about this enhancement before thinking about it.

Magnesium

One of the symptoms of low magnesium levels in your body is rest issues. This mineral is the fundamental fixing in Mag Three, is associated with many body cycles and assumes a significant part in bone wellbeing, heart wellbeing, and cerebrum capability. Stress, tragically, may bring about your magnesium levels dropping. This causes a decrease in cerebrum synthetic creation, including your melatonin, consequently disturbing your regular circadian musicality. Taking into account magnesium as one of the regular items for rest support a sleeping disorder may in this manner assist with correcting your body's magnesium levels as well as help with the development of the cerebrum synthetic substances that guarantee a decent night's rest. Do know that a magnesium supplement might cause issues, queasiness, and looseness of the bowels. Individuals experiencing specific medical issue like kidney infection should likewise not accept it as an enhancement without first conversing with their medical services professional. Ingesting too much magnesium, albeit interesting, is conceivable. Side effects of a magnesium glut incorporate exhaustion, low circulatory strain, looseness of the bowels, and muscle shortcoming. It could likewise possibly be deadly.

Cannabidiol (CBD)

CBD is one of the cannabinoids found in the marijuana plant. In contrast to tetrahydrocannabinol (THC) which is psychoactive and gets you the run of the mill high connected with marijuana, CBD doesn't give this impact. All things being equal, working with your body's endocannabinoid framework, CBD assists your body with keeping a condition of equilibrium. CBD at present has numerous applications like Canna Emollient and Canna Splash, it is additionally noted for giving alleviation in individual's epilepsy. Research additionally shows that CBD might decrease nervousness and advance rest. No proof recommends you can go too far with CBD although you might encounter a dry mouth, sluggishness, and discombobulation. Certain individuals may likewise see a bringing down in their circulatory strain.

Chamomile

Chamomile has, for quite a while, been on the rundown of regular items for rest support a sleeping disorder. This might be because of the presence of apigenin, a flavonoid that ties to your cerebrum's benzodiazepine receptors. Chamomile, as indicated by research, may likewise have pressure diminishing properties, along these lines advancing rest. Albeit for the most part thought to be protected, recommended individuals have/had malignant growth, endometriosis, or uterine fibroids or who experience the ill effects of dust sensitivities shouldn't do as such without first counseling their medical services professional. It might likewise slow down the viability of anti-conception medication pills.

Valerian Root

Valerian roots and tea eases nervousness, has a quieting impact, and advances relaxing rest. It appears to act in a similar design as a narcotic. Albeit considered alright for transient use, the enhancement might make a few side impacts. These incorporate cerebral pains, an irritated stomach, heart palpitations, dry mouth, and now and again, expanded nervousness. Valerian root may likewise neutralize the effectiveness of specific prescriptions.

Lavender

Lavender is a Mediterranean plant that has spread to all landmasses. Found in many nurseries across the globe, the aroma might improve your rest. Various investigations support this. It might likewise ease nervousness and discouragement. Lavender is considered most likely safe when taken inside in prescription measurements and ought to presumably not be utilized straightforwardly previously or after medical procedure. This is because it might dial back your focal sensory system and, joined with prescriptions and sedation, may dial it back something over the top.

Enthusiasm Blossom

Research shows the enthusiasm blossom might have hostile to nervousness properties and may assist with tending to a sleeping disorder. This it might do by supporting your cerebrum GABA that outcomes in less mind movement and along these lines advancing rest. Albeit for the most part thought to be protected, incidental effects incorporate discombobulation and disarray. It might likewise expand the impacts of sedation, so it ought not to be utilized preceding an activity.

THE SIGNIFICANCE OF A DECENT NIGHT'S REST

Many individuals feel they work well on a couple of hours' rest an evening. At the end of the day, over the long haul, your wellbeing can begin to endure. Your cerebrum's NeuroEndoMetabolic (NEM) stress reaction is your body's protection instrument against pressure of any sort. Your Neuroaffect Circuit is important for the NEM and comprises of your cerebrum, your autonomic sensory system, and your microbiome. At the point when you are exposed to pressure, your cerebrum promptly gets a move on sends substance couriers to different pieces of your body to carry it into preparation to one or the other battle or escape. This outcomes in an expansion in pressure chemicals that influences all chemicals and body processes. When the pressure is gone, your cerebrum reestablishes ordinary capability to all parts impacted. At the point when stress is drawn out, ordinary capability isn't reestablished. This implies that processes that were delayed down or stopped, remain as such. This might prompt different medical problems and, because of the effect on your adrenal organs, adrenal exhaustion. The effect on your cerebrum is galactic.

Your cerebrum is reliant upon different chemicals that go about as synthetic couriers, for example synapses. These are most frequently as chemicals. Because of progressing pressure, your different cerebrum chemicals' creation might decline. This could have a serious effect on different body capabilities as well as on cerebrum capability too. Nervousness, discouragement, and rest issues, for example, a sleeping disorder might result.

PART 8 – BIPOLAR DISORDER AND THE KETO ASSIST METHOD

Bipolar disorder can disturb all aspects of your life, including your work and your connections. Medication and talk treatment can assist with controlling the serious high and low changes in state of mind, discouragement, and craziness side effects. You could have additionally thought to be attempting elective treatments, similar to consume less calories changes. Albeit changing your eating routine won't fix bipolar confusion, there is some proof that specific food decisions can help. One eating regimen specifically, the ketogenic diet, can help individuals with this condition, as indicated by restricted research.

WHAT IS THE KETOGENIC DIET?

The ketogenic diet has been around since the 1920s. It's a high-fat, low-starch diet that impersonates the express your body would go into on the off chance that you were fasting. Ordinarily, starches, to be specific glucose, supply your body and cerebrum with energy. Glucose is the cerebrum's favored wellspring of fuel. At the point when you cut carbs from your cating routine, fat takes over as your body's essential energy source. The liver separates fats into substances called ketones, which are normally higher in energy than starches. Ketones venture out through your circulatory system to fuel your cerebrum.

There are two varieties of the eating routine:

- On the exemplary ketogenic diet, you eat a proportion of 3:1 to 5:1 fats to protein in addition to starches. At the end of the day, three to multiple times how much fat contrasted with protein and carbs consolidated. The greater part of your eating routine is comprised of fats from food varieties like fish, for example, sardines and salmon, margarine, red meat, avocado, chicken, eggs, cheddar, coconut milk, seeds, and nuts. The vast majority of your carbs come from vegetables.

- On the medium-chain fatty substance (MCT) diet, you get around 60% of your complete calories from a kind of coconut oil. You can eat more protein and carbs on the MCT diet than you would have the option to on the exemplary ketogenic diet.

Hostile to seizure prescriptions, similar medications used to treat individuals with epilepsy, are installations of bipolar problem treatment. This made specialists keep thinking about whether an eating routine that assists with epilepsy side effects could likewise assist individuals with bipolar confusion. There's motivation to accept it can. During a depressed or hyper episode, energy creation eases back in the cerebrum. Eating a ketogenic diet can increment energy in the cerebrum. Individuals with bipolar confusion have higher-than-ordinary measures of sodium inside their cells. Lithium and other state of mind balancing out drugs used to treat bipolar confusion work, to a limited extent, by bringing down sodium levels in cells. The ketogenic diet

Has a similar sort of impact. However the ketogenic diet is promising for bipolar confusion, there isn't any firm proof that it works. The eating routine is exceptionally restricted, so it can prompt lacks in specific supplements, like nutrients B, C, and D, as well as calcium, magnesium, and iron. Certain individuals additionally foster an adjustment of breath scent, energy levels, and disagreeable stomach related side effects, similar to queasiness, regurgitating, and obstruction. In uncommon cases, the eating regimen has prompted more serious secondary effects, like unusual heart rhythms, pancreatitis, debilitated bones, and kidney stones. In this manner, somebody following a ketogenic diet ought to expect to eat great food varieties for bipolar confusion, like the accompanying:

- Meats - hamburger, sheep, fish, poultry, and eggs
- Vegetables - hold back nothing "ground" veggies, like broccoli and cauliflower, and salad greens like kale and spinach
- High-fat dairy - margarine, cream, and hard cheeses
- Nuts/Seeds - the most ideal choices while following a bipolar ketogenic diet are macadamias, sunflower seeds, and pecans
- Sound fat - avocado and coconut oil are both extraordinary wellsprings of solid fat
- Similarly as there are sure food varieties to remember for a ketogenic diet for bipolar confusion, there are likewise some to keep away from (or if nothing else decline admission of) including:
- Wheat - a keto diet for bipolar confusion is low in starches, so staying away from things like pasta, bread, and cereal is suggested
- Starch - potatoes, vegetables, and beans are all in the starch family, and to be stayed away from
- Natural product - high in sugar and carbs, most natural product is to be stayed away from on this eating routine

Dietary changes can be troublesome, and results might take time. In any case, on the off chance that you are searching for a characteristic method for treating or potentially deal with your bipolar problem side effects, attempting a ketogenic diet might be valuable. In any case, assuming you are taking bipolar prescription, it is essential to note bipolar weight control plans that are exceptionally low in starches can influence and modify how the medicine is handled in the body. Along these lines, looking for clinical advice is enthusiastically suggested.

PART 9- FENUGREEK; THE LIBIDO MAGIC SPICE OR MORE

Fenugreek is a spice that is additionally ordinarily alluded to as Trigonella foenum-graecum. The seeds are much of the time found in groceries, for example, fixings or utilized straightforwardly in cooking, especially in dishes that are connected with the Southern and Focal districts of Asia. Furthermore, it has been around since roughly 4000BC and follows tracked down in the burial chamber of Tutankhamen. Fenugreek was a generally involved restorative plant in spots like Europe and the USA, yet it is as yet well known in India. This is reflected by India's situation similar to the biggest maker of fenugreek on the planet. The seeds in all actuality do have some dietary benefit; they are exceptionally high in iron substance in addition to protein and fiber. However there's likewise almost 50% of your suggested day to day portion of magnesium, in addition to over a fourth of your requirements for vitamin B6, a sound measure of potassium despite more modest measures of L-ascorbic acid, vitamin A, and calcium. These figures are fascinating because those nutrients and minerals have proof to exhibit they are valuable towards delivering a sound measure of testosterone which can assist with combatting age related andropause.

Furthermore, research shows the way that fenugreek can likewise assist with the freeing the impacts from the menopause. In this way, as a speedy outline of fenugreek, we can see there's a great deal of history, a ton of purpose and it has some strong healthy benefit. However, let us take a gander at its advantages for charisma, in the two guys and females in addition to the necessary portions If we separate it to its exceptionally crude reason, moxie is a capability to reproduce and make due as an animal categories. Charisma itself is one of numerous areas that comprise of ordinary sexual capability and intercourse. Having a low charisma can add to a diminished longing for sex and the capacity to have sex. Research recommends that this sexual craving and need to have sex is altogether different among people. They say that men have a higher sex drive and it is more direct. Though, the idea is that ladies will quite often put more worth on social, ecological, and feeling. What they additionally cover is that no individual's sex drive or charisma is something very similar. This longing for sexual movement is impacted by various variables, and for the most part shouldn't be visible as an 'on-off' instrument. It has been talked about that the various variables impacting charisma can go from natural, mental, life conditions, prescriptions, and social circumstances.

CHARISMA CHANGES

We have proactively addressed the various variables that can impact an individual's sex drive and charisma. While charisma is the instrument to reproduce, some appear to profoundly want to do as such than others. Once more, this is ordinary as everybody is unique. Notwithstanding, we should investigate the regions that can cause charisma changes for an individual;

Charisma and Age

Indeed, age. It gets us all in the long run. Notwithstanding, it is unquestionably hypothesized that a male's charisma is normally expanded during their youngsters, which corresponds with pubescence and the convergence of expanded testosterone creation. This pinnacle in the long run tails off after some time however seems to make an unexpected spike of sexual craving. Then again, when females arrive at pubescence in their youngsters, they experience a more slow increment of sexual craving until they arrive at their thirties when it pinnacles and in this manner drives female charisma.

Charisma and Menopause

On the off chance that we simply return to a definitive justification behind charisma: the need to reproduce. It will not shock hear that a lady will in general hit top sexual craving not long before ovulation. This period is the point at which a lady is at her most noteworthy place of fruitfulness. Be that as it may, when a lady enters her menopausal stage, this denotes the moment that she would quit having her period, ovulate and have the option to become pregnant. Normally, as a lady can never again ovulate and isn't prolific, the fundamental or regular requirement for charisma decreases, this is likewise joined by a decrease in testosterone which additionally adds to a diminished moxie. This is joined by vaginal dryness and experience torment during sex.

Charisma and Chemicals

Chemicals are significant for both male and female charisma.

Testosterone

There is an unmistakable relationship amongst testosterone and a sound charisma. A deficiency of charisma, especially in men is related with the regular downfall of testosterone that is ordinarily alluded to as the andropause.

Estrogen

Furthermore, ladies likewise need to deliver estrogen to make a good overall arrangement of sex chemicals to keep up with sexual longing as well as advancing vaginal grease. Be that as it may, ladies are dependent upon numerous hormonal changes all through their lives which can disturb this equilibrium, and, thusly, influence their charisma. Men expect estrogen to keep up with charisma also. While it is challenging to decide the equilibrium expected among estrogen and testosterone, there is proof (some clashing) that estrogen emphatically affects charisma in men.

Charisma and liquor

Men might have known about the 'brewers hang'. This is a term begat in light of the impact liquor can have on charisma and result in erectile brokenness. Be that as it may, liquor in all actuality does likewise influence ladies. It is accounted for that it might increment emotional sexual craving while diminishes excitement and sexual capability.

Depression

Depression is a difficult sickness that adversely affects numerous parts of an individual's life. Having a diminished charisma is one of the side effects of discouragement, alongside sensations of sadness and losing the interest of delight in things that were once delighted in. Furthermore, antidepressants can likewise cause an indifference or want in sex.

Work out

Another region that requires balance. No or exceptionally low degrees of activity can prompt infections like corpulence, diabetes, and malignant growths. This has displayed to increment sexual brokenness among all kinds of people. Proof presents serious areas of strength for a between actual wellness/practice with worked on sexual capability. Notwithstanding, there is likewise proof that those engaged with challenging and outrageous episodes of perseverance exercise can likewise prompt a decreased charisma.

Stress

Many individuals experience tension during their everyday lives. This pressure can prompt contracted supply routes which can influence blood stream and thusly guarantee erectile brokenness. Moreover, the individuals who experience the ill effects of PTSD, especially those veterans of military assistance experience sexual brokenness of up to multiple times that of those without PTSD.

THE MOST EFFECTIVE METHOD TO EXPAND YOUR CHARISMA NORMALLY

In many regards, where potential, we want to address the regions addressed which are known to kill charisma. All things considered, on the off chance that your activity levels are low, increment them however not to the place where you are subscribing to outrageous perseverance accomplishments. Another region is to decrease liquor utilization on the off chance that your levels are high and it is having an adverse consequence. On the off chance that conceivable, treatment and exhortation ought to be looked for discouragement and stress. Furthermore, we can likewise search out regular aphrodisiacs. These can be food varieties, spices, plants, or seeds. A Spanish fly is something that can stimulate sexual intuition, increment want and delight. It need not simply be something to be consumed and can be visual or material.

ARE CHARISMA ENHANCEMENTS SAFE?

It is challenging to state whether all charisma supplements are protected, that is because there is no set supplement profile for moxie supplements. One item can tremendously contrast from one more with regards to the included fixings. Be that as it may, fenugreek is by and large safe for a great many people with any issues for the most part encompassing gastrointestinal inconvenience as opposed to some other issues. This is except if you are pregnant. Moreover, fenugreek might collaborate for certain different prescriptions. There's some worry that it might increment blood diminishing when taken close by medications like warfarin or decrease glucose levels an excessive amount of when joined with hypoglycemic specialists. A further focal point is the stringy substance of fenugreek might significantly affect the ingestion of any prescriptions that you are taking, and in this manner it is encouraged to take anything containing fenugreek something like 2 hours earlier. If you in all actuality do experience the ill effects of sensitivities of peanuts, soybeans and chickpeas you might wish to keep away from fenugreek as there could be a reactivity because of them having similar Fabaceae group of vegetables/peas/beans. Ladies who are at present experiencing chemical delicate malignant growths shouldn't utilize fenugreek supplements.

Fenugreek Advantages for Men
- Sperm Wellbeing
- Muscle and Strength

Fenugreek Advantages for Ladies
- Lactation
- Period Torments and Spasms
- Fenugreek for charisma

Different Advantages of Fenugreek
- Type 2 Diabetes
- Satiety
- Diminishing Fat Mass
- Cardiovascular Infection
- Going bald
- Dermatology

OTHER DIFFERENT APHRODISIACS THAT MIGHT SUPPORT YOUR CHARISMA

Maca

Maca is a sweet root vegetable with a few medical advantages. In South America, individuals ordinarily use it to support fruitfulness, and its epithet is "the Peruvian Viagra." It fills for the most part in the mountains of focal Peru and is connected with cruciferous vegetables, including broccoli, cauliflower, kale, and cabbage. Creature concentrates on tracked down expansions in charisma and erectile capability in rodents in the wake of consuming Maca. Four different examinations recommend it might support charisma in people, as well. One little review has demonstrated that maca may assist with diminishing the deficiency of charisma that ordinarily happens as a symptom of specific stimulant medications. Most investigations gave 1.5-3.5 grams of maca each day for 2-12 weeks. Members for the most part endured these admissions well and experienced not many incidental effects. Be that as it may, more investigations are expected to decide safe measurements and long haul impacts.

Tribulus

Tribulus terrestris, otherwise called *bindii*, is a yearly plant that fills in dry environments. Makers of enhancements frequently guarantee that it can support charisma. Review have recommended that it might bring testosterone steps up in certain creatures, however science hasn't demonstrated that it can increment testosterone levels or fruitfulness in people. Restricted proof recommends it might assist with supporting sexual capability and want in guys and females.

Ginkgo biloba

Ginkgo biloba is a home grown supplement got from one of the most established types of trees — the Ginkgo biloba tree. Conventional Chinese medication utilizes it to treat numerous infirmities, including discouragement and poor sexual capability. Ginkgo biloba is said to go about as a sexual enhancer by loosening up veins and increment blood stream. All things considered, studies have delivered blended results. In 1998, for instance, a little report detailed that ginkgo biloba diminished the deficiency of charisma that stimulant utilize caused in around 84% of members. Both male and female members said they encountered expanded want, energy and capacity to climax in the wake of consuming 60-240 mg of the enhancement day to day, although impacts appeared to be more grounded in female members. Be that as it may, this was an inferior quality review, and its discoveries may not be dependable. A more thorough subsequent review was distributed in 2004. This study found no enhancements in a comparative gathering of members who took ginkgo biloba. Ginkgo biloba is for the most part very much endured, however it might go about as a blood more slender. Along these lines, if you're taking blood-diminishing prescriptions, make a point to check with your medical services supplier before taking ginkgo biloba.

Red ginseng

Ginseng is one more well-known spice in Chinese medication. One specific sort — red ginseng — is ordinarily used to treat different afflictions in people, including low charisma and sexual capability. A few investigations have seen that red ginseng is more successful than a fake treatment at working on erectile capability. Additionally, one little investigation discovered that red ginseng might work on sexual excitement during menopause. Be that as it may, these outcomes are not all inclusive, and a few specialists question the strength of these investigations. They caution that more examination is required before serious areas of strength for making. Most investigations had members take 1.8-3 grams of red ginseng day to day for 4-12 weeks. Individuals for the most part endure ginseng well, however it might slow down blood-diminishing prescriptions and the therapy of chemical delicate malignant growths. Now and again, ginseng may likewise cause cerebral pains, obstruction, or minor stomach upset.

Pistachio nuts

Individuals have been eating pistachio nuts since 6,000 B.C. They have dietary benefit and are wealthy in protein, fiber, and solid fats. Pistachios might have an assortment of medical advantages, including assisting lower with blooding pressure, oversee weight, and decrease the gamble of coronary illness. They may likewise assist with diminishing side effects of erectile brokenness. In one little review, guys who consumed 3.5 ounces (100 grams) of pistachio nuts each day for a considerable length of time experienced expanded blood stream to the penis and firmer erections.

Saffron

Saffron is a flavor gotten from the Crocus sativus blossom. It's local to Southwest Asia and one of the most costly flavors by weight. This flavor is much of the time utilized as an elective solution for assist with treating discouragement, diminish pressure, and upgrade state of mind. Saffron is additionally well known for its expected sexual enhancer properties, particularly in people taking antidepressants. All things considered, concentrates on saffron's sexual enhancer properties in people without discouragement yield conflicting outcomes.

THE PRIMARY CONCERN

With regards to supporting sex drive, the rundown of food varieties with potential Spanish fly properties is extremely lengthy. Be that as it may, just a little extent of these alleged aphrodisiacs are supported by science. On the off chance that you're keen on checking the science-supported choices out, you might need to begin with limited quantities and increment the measurements in light of your resistance. Additionally, it's essential to take note of that regular aphrodisiacs might collaborate for certain prescriptions. If you're at present taking prescription, make a point to check with your medical services supplier before checking these food varieties and spices out.

PART 10- THE COOKING EXERCISE AS A BRAIN AID

On the off chance that you feel comfortable in the kitchen, arranging and getting ready nutritious dinners, congrats! You're not just refueling your body; you're invigorating your cerebrum with the sort of exercise it requirements to stay solid. Delivering an occasion supper with every one of the decorations will unquestionably burden your leader working, however more limited size dinners request comparable abilities:

- Figuring out a dinner plan, maybe by exploring recipes on the web or in cookbooks, constrains you to expect and coordinate.
- Calculating subtleties into your preparation - your sibling despises green beans, you served an Italian dish the last opportunity he came over - expects you to recollect and to take care of issues as you endeavor to plan a menu that will fulfill everybody.
- Making a rundown and looking for everyday food items draws on memory and concentration. On the off chance that every one of the fixings you want are not accessible, you might need to make do, which additionally helps your cerebrum.
- Performing multiple tasks and coordinating become possibly the most important factor as you set up the dinner to guarantee that all that you're serving is prepared simultaneously.
- Leader capability applies to another aspect: overseeing dissatisfaction and controlling feelings. You might need to draw on these mental assets on the off chance that your feast arrangement turns out badly or your supper crashes and burns, notwithstanding your earnest attempts. Try not to surrender. Effortlessness under tension is only another indication of a solid cerebrum!

We've all accomplished the delight and quiet of cooking, however is there a science behind the psychological well-being advantages of the pleasant side interest? The response is yes. Cooking is turning out to be increasingly more typical as a treatment for a wide assortment of conduct medical issue like ADHD, dietary problems, nervousness, and discouragement.

Ayurvedic medication has been showing us for a long time that there is serious areas of strength for a between psychological well-being and diet, however when you consolidate that with the demonstration of truly picking, planning and preparing the food yourself, the arrangement ends up being self-evident and a normally more grounded identity creates. While you're cooking, you're at the time. You're getting the tomato, cutting it down the center, feeling the impression of juice running down your hand, lastly tasting that scrumptious new natural product as it supports your body. This large number of sensations can provide you with a more noteworthy feeling of presence, and that permits you to see the value in every second for what it is, which thusly provides you with a more noteworthy feeling of satisfaction.

Furthermore, when you initiate the right side (the more imaginative side) of the cerebrum, you are connecting with an alternate piece of your mind that you could ordinarily underuse during the day, and this likewise can energize a more powerful utilization of cells.

The cerebrum is basically a muscle, and the more we utilize that odd muscle again and again we end up with a more grounded generally speaking outcome. So whether it's a feeling of satisfaction or a more powerful psyche that you're later, you ought to flip through certain recipes and reach for the good old spatula. You'll be astonished at the feeling of quiet cooking can give — keep in mind, smoothies don't count.

END AND SYNOPSIS

Eat Extraordinary Cerebrum Foods!!!!!

Food varieties that contain high measures of cancer prevention agents assist your body and cerebrum with remaining youthful. A few examinations have found that eating food wealthy in cell reinforcements, which incorporate many products of the soil, fundamentally diminishes the gamble of creating mental debilitation. Eat foods grown from the ground of various varieties to guarantee that you are getting a wide assortment of cell reinforcements to support and safeguard your cerebrum. The following is a rundown of extraordinary cerebrum food.

Excellent Cerebrum Food varieties

- Crude Almonds
- Almond Milk (unsweetened)
- Apples
- Asparagus
- Avocados
- Bananas
- Beans (dark, pinto, garbanzo)
- Ringer Peppers
- Beets
- Blackberries
- Blueberries
- Broccoli
- Brussel sprouts
- Carrots
- Cheddar (low-fat)
- Cherries
- Chicken (skinless)
- Cranberries
- Egg whites (DHA advanced)
- Grapefruit
- Herring
- Honeydew
- Kiwi
- Lemons
- Lentils
- Limes
- Oats
- Olives
- Olive oil
- Oranges
- Peaches

- Peas
- Plums
- Pomegranates
- Raspberries
- Red grapes
- Soybeans
- Spinach
- Strawberries
- Green Tea
- Tofu
- Tomatoes
- Fish
- Turkey (skinless)
- Pecans
- Water
- Entire Wheat
- Wild salmon
- Sweet potato and yams
- Yogurt (unsweetened)